C. B. BRODOSKI
Negotiation Methods And Tactics

First published by True Northwest Publishing 2024

Copyright © 2024 by C. B. Brodoski

All rights reserved. No part of this publication may be reproduced, stored or transmitted in any form or by any means, electronic, mechanical, photocopying, recording, scanning, or otherwise without written permission from the publisher. It is illegal to copy this book, post it to a website, or distribute it by any other means without permission.

C. B. Brodoski asserts the moral right to be identified as the author of this work.

C. B. Brodoski has no responsibility for the persistence or accuracy of URLs for external or third-party Internet Websites referred to in this publication and does not guarantee that any content on such Websites is, or will remain, accurate or appropriate.

Designations used by companies to distinguish their products are often claimed as trademarks. All brand names and product names used in this book and on its cover are trade names, service marks, trademarks and registered trademarks of their respective owners. The publishers and the book are not associated with any product or vendor mentioned in this book. None of the companies referenced within the book have endorsed the book.

First edition

This book was professionally typeset on Reedsy.
Find out more at reedsy.com

Dedication
To the brave men and women of law enforcement and first responders,
This book is dedicated to you—the courageous individuals who stand on the front lines every day, protecting our communities and keeping us safe. Your unwavering commitment, selflessness, and dedication to duty inspire us all.

Contents

Introduction	1
Introduction	1
Chapter 1	6
Chapter 1: Fundamentals of Police Negotiation	6
Chapter 2	12
Chapter 2: Preparing for Negotiation	12
Chapter 3	19
Chapter 3: Crisis Negotiation	19
Chapter 4	27
Chapter 4: Tactical Communication Skills	27
Chapter 5	35
Chapter 5: Specialized Negotiation Scenarios	35
Domestic Violence Situations	35
Mental Health Crises	37
Terrorism and Extremism	38
Negotiating with Organized Crime	39
Kidnapping and Ransom Situations	41
Chapter 6	43
Chapter 6: Building and Leading a Negotiation Team	43
Team Structure and Roles	43
Leadership and Team Dynamics	45
Training and Development	46
Coordination with Other Units	48
Chapter 7	50

Chapter 7: Technological Tools in Negotiation — 50
   Communication Technology — 50
   Surveillance and Intelligence Gathering — 52
   Data Analysis and Decision Support — 54
   Technological Innovations — 55
Chapter 8 — 57
   Chapter 8: Ethical and Legal Considerations — 57
   Legal Framework for Negotiation — 57
   Ethical Principles in Negotiation — 59
   Accountability and Transparency — 61
   Cultural Sensitivity and Diversity — 62
Chapter 9 — 64
   Chapter 9: Post-Negotiation Analysis — 64
   Debriefing and Evaluation — 64
   Learning from Successes and Failures — 66
   Psychological Impact on Negotiators — 67
   Creating a Knowledge Base — 68
Chapter 10 — 71
   Chapter 10: Conclusion — 71
   Summary of Key Points — 71
   Future Trends in Police Negotiation — 73
   Final Thoughts — 74

Introduction

Introduction

Negotiation Methods and Tactics:

1. Purpose of the Book

Negotiation lies at the heart of effective law enforcement, where the ability to communicate, de-escalate, and resolve conflicts peacefully is not just a skill but a necessity. This book serves as a comprehensive guide designed to equip law enforcement professionals with the knowledge, strategies, and practical techniques essential for successful negotiation in diverse and challenging scenarios.

Goals and Objectives

The primary goal of this book is to provide a structured approach to negotiation specifically tailored for law enforcement contexts. It aims to:

- **Educate and Inform**: By exploring fundamental concepts and advanced strategies, this book aims to enhance the understanding of negotiation principles among law enforcement officers.
- **Equip with Practical Skills**: Provide practical tools and techniques that can be applied in real-world situations to achieve peaceful resolutions while ensuring public safety.

- **Promote Ethical Practices**: Emphasize the importance of ethical behavior and professionalism in negotiation, maintaining trust and integrity within communities.

Importance of Understanding Negotiation in Police Work

Negotiation skills are pivotal in law enforcement for several reasons:

- **Enhancing Public Safety**: Effective negotiation can prevent escalations, minimize the use of force, and protect the lives of civilians, officers, and suspects alike.
- **Building Community Trust**: Ethical and effective negotiation fosters positive relationships between law enforcement and the community, promoting cooperation and support.
- **Professional Development**: Mastery of negotiation techniques enhances the overall effectiveness and professionalism of law enforcement officers, contributing to successful outcomes in challenging situations.

Overview of What the Reader Will Learn

This book covers a wide array of topics essential for mastering negotiation in law enforcement:

- **Fundamental Principles**: Understanding the basics of negotiation, including communication strategies, psychological insights, and tactical approaches.
- **Advanced Techniques**: Exploring specialized negotiation techniques for crisis situations, hostage negotiations, and complex scenarios.
- **Technological Integration**: Discussing the role of technology

in modern negotiation, including communication platforms, data analytics, and virtual reality.
- **Ethical Considerations**: Addressing ethical dilemmas and promoting ethical decision-making in negotiation processes.

2. The Role of Negotiation in Law Enforcement

Historical Context

Negotiation in law enforcement has evolved significantly over the decades, transitioning from a reactive to a proactive approach aimed at conflict resolution and crisis management. Historical case studies illustrate the evolution of tactics and strategies employed by law enforcement agencies worldwide.

The Evolution of Negotiation Tactics

From early hostage crises to contemporary negotiations involving diverse and dynamic threats, law enforcement tactics have adapted to meet new challenges. Advances in training, technology, and understanding of human behavior have shaped the evolution of negotiation strategies.

Case Studies of Successful Negotiations

Examining real-life cases where negotiation techniques led to successful outcomes provides valuable insights and practical lessons. These case studies highlight the application of negotiation principles in various high-stakes scenarios, demonstrating the effectiveness of structured approaches and strategic decision-making.

3. Structure of the Book

Brief Description of Each Chapter

- **Chapter 1: Fundamentals of Police Negotiation**: Introduces basic negotiation concepts, the importance of negotiation skills in law enforcement, and psychological principles relevant to negotiation.

- **Chapter 2: The Role of Negotiation in Law Enforcement**: Explores the historical context, evolution of tactics, and case studies of successful negotiations in law enforcement.
- **Chapter 3: Communication Strategies**: Discusses effective communication techniques, active listening, and verbal de-escalation methods crucial for negotiation success.
- **Chapter 4: Psychological Insights**: Examines behavioral analysis, crisis intervention strategies, and cognitive biases impacting negotiation outcomes.
- **Chapter 5: Advanced Negotiation Techniques**: Covers specialized techniques for crisis negotiations, hostage situations, and complex scenarios.
- **Chapter 6: Technological Tools in Negotiation**: Explores the integration of technology, including communication platforms, data analytics, and virtual reality, in enhancing negotiation effectiveness.
- **Chapter 7: Ethical Considerations**: Addresses ethical dilemmas, principles of ethical negotiation, and maintaining professionalism and integrity in law enforcement.
- **Chapter 8: Training and Preparation**: Discusses the importance of training programs, simulation exercises, and ongoing professional development for negotiators.
- **Chapter 9: Case Studies and Analysis**: Analyzes additional case studies, applying learned principles and techniques to real-world scenarios.
- **Chapter 10: Future Trends in Negotiation**: Explores emerging trends, technological advancements, and evolving practices shaping the future of negotiation in law enforcement.

How to Use This Book

This book is designed to be a practical resource for law enforcement professionals at all levels of experience:

- **Self-Study**: Officers can read through chapters sequentially to build a comprehensive understanding of negotiation principles and techniques.
- **Training Resource**: Training officers and instructors can use specific chapters as modules for in-service training and professional development programs.
- **Reference Guide**: Experienced negotiators can refer to specific chapters or sections for insights and strategies applicable to current or upcoming negotiations.

By integrating the knowledge and skills presented in this book into their practice, law enforcement officers can enhance their ability to effectively manage crises, resolve conflicts peacefully, and uphold public safety with professionalism and integrity.

Chapter 1

Chapter 1: Fundamentals of Police Negotiation

Effective negotiation is a cornerstone of modern law enforcement, providing a peaceful means to resolve conflicts, manage crises, and ensure the safety of all parties involved. This chapter explores the fundamentals of police negotiation, offering a comprehensive understanding of its definition, importance, psychological underpinnings, and basic framework.

What is Police Negotiation?

Definition and Scope

Police negotiation is a specialized field within law enforcement focused on resolving situations through dialogue and communication rather than physical force. It encompasses a wide range of scenarios, including hostage situations, barricaded suspects, suicidal individuals, and other high-stress incidents where peaceful resolution is paramount. The scope of police negotiation extends beyond crisis situations to include everyday interactions with the public, where effective communication can de-escalate potential conflicts.

Key Concepts and Terminology

Chapter 1

To understand police negotiation, it is essential to familiarize oneself with key concepts and terminology:

- **Crisis Negotiation**: A specific type of police negotiation aimed at resolving situations where there is an immediate threat to life or safety.
- **Hostage Negotiation**: A subset of crisis negotiation dealing specifically with scenarios where individuals are held against their will.
- **De-escalation**: Techniques used to reduce the intensity of a conflict or potentially violent situation.
- **Rapport Building**: The process of establishing a relationship of trust and understanding between the negotiator and the subject.
- **Active Listening**: A communication technique that involves giving full attention to the speaker, understanding their message, and responding thoughtfully.

The Importance of Negotiation Skills in Policing

Building Rapport and Trust

One of the most critical aspects of police negotiation is the ability to build rapport and trust with the individuals involved. This involves:

- **Empathy**: Demonstrating genuine concern and understanding of the subject's feelings and perspective.
- **Respect**: Treating the subject with dignity, regardless of the circumstances.
- **Honesty**: Being truthful in communication to build credibility and trust.

Building rapport can lead to more open communication, making it easier to understand the subject's needs and motivations, which is crucial for finding a peaceful resolution.

De-escalation Techniques

De-escalation is a vital skill in policing, aimed at reducing the intensity of a situation without resorting to force. Effective de-escalation techniques include:

- **Calm Communication**: Using a calm and steady tone of voice to reassure and pacify the subject.
- **Non-Threatening Body Language**: Adopting an open and non-aggressive stance to avoid escalating tensions.
- **Active Listening**: Paying close attention to the subject's words and emotions, reflecting their concerns, and validating their feelings.

De-escalation techniques help prevent situations from spiraling out of control, protecting both law enforcement officers and the public.

Reducing the Use of Force

One of the primary goals of police negotiation is to minimize the need for physical force. By effectively communicating and negotiating, officers can often persuade subjects to comply voluntarily, reducing the risk of injury or death. This not only ensures the safety of all parties but also promotes a more positive relationship between law enforcement and the community.

Psychological Principles of Negotiation

Understanding Human Behavior

Effective negotiation requires a deep understanding of human behavior. Key psychological principles that influence negotiation include:

- **Motivation**: Understanding what drives the subject's actions and

decisions.
- **Perception**: Recognizing how the subject views the situation, which may differ significantly from the objective reality.
- **Emotions**: Identifying and managing emotions, both in the subject and the negotiator, to maintain control of the situation.

The Psychology of Crisis Situations

Crisis situations are characterized by heightened emotions, stress, and often irrational behavior. Understanding the psychological dynamics at play can help negotiators manage these situations more effectively. Key factors include:

- **Fight or Flight Response**: Recognizing that subjects may be operating under intense fear or anger, influencing their actions.
- **Cognitive Overload**: Realizing that high-stress situations can impair the subject's ability to think clearly and make rational decisions.
- **Need for Control**: Many subjects in crisis situations feel a loss of control, and negotiators can help by offering choices and empowering the subject in small ways.

Cognitive Biases and Their Impact

Cognitive biases are systematic patterns of deviation from norm or rationality in judgment, which can impact negotiation. Key biases to be aware of include:

- **Confirmation Bias**: The tendency to search for, interpret, and remember information that confirms one's preconceptions.
- **Anchoring Bias**: Relying too heavily on the first piece of information encountered (the "anchor") when making decisions.
- **Availability Heuristic**: Overestimating the importance of infor-

mation that is readily available or recent.

By understanding and mitigating these biases, negotiators can make more informed and balanced decisions.

Basic Negotiation Framework

Phases of Negotiation

Effective negotiation typically follows a structured process, divided into distinct phases:

1. **Preparation**: Gathering information, assessing risks, and establishing a negotiation team.
2. **Initial Contact**: Making contact with the subject, establishing communication, and beginning rapport building.
3. **Engagement**: Actively negotiating, exploring options, and working towards a resolution.
4. **Resolution**: Reaching an agreement or solution, and ensuring the safe conclusion of the situation.
5. **Debriefing**: Reviewing the negotiation process, outcomes, and lessons learned to improve future performance.

Goals and Objectives

The primary goals of police negotiation are:

- **Safety**: Ensuring the safety of all individuals involved, including hostages, subjects, and officers.
- **Resolution**: Achieving a peaceful resolution to the situation.
- **Compliance**: Persuading the subject to comply with law enforcement directives.

CHAPTER 1

Common Strategies and Tactics
Negotiators employ various strategies and tactics to achieve these goals, including:

- **Building Trust**: Establishing credibility and trustworthiness with the subject.
- **Offering Options**: Providing alternatives that allow the subject to feel a sense of control and choice.
- **Using Time**: Recognizing that time can be an ally, allowing emotions to settle and rational thinking to prevail.
- **Leveraging Relationships**: Involving family members, friends, or trusted individuals who can influence the subject positively.

Conclusion

The fundamentals of police negotiation encompass a wide range of skills, knowledge, and psychological insights. By understanding the definition and scope of negotiation, the importance of building rapport and trust, the psychological principles at play, and the basic framework of negotiation, law enforcement officers can approach these situations with confidence and competence. The subsequent chapters will delve deeper into each aspect, providing a comprehensive guide to mastering negotiation methods and tactics in law enforcement.

Chapter 2

Chapter 2: Preparing for Negotiation

Effective negotiation in law enforcement requires meticulous preparation. The success of a negotiation often hinges on the groundwork laid before the actual dialogue begins. This chapter delves into the critical aspects of pre-negotiation planning, understanding the situation, developing a strategy, and the importance of role-playing and simulation exercises.

Pre-Negotiation Planning

Gathering Intelligence and Information

The first step in any negotiation is to gather as much information as possible about the situation, individuals involved, and any relevant background details. This intelligence forms the foundation for all subsequent negotiation tactics and decisions. Information can be gathered from various sources, including:

- **Background Checks**: Understanding the history of the individuals involved, including any criminal records, psychological evaluations, and previous encounters with law enforcement.

- **Witness Statements**: Collecting accounts from witnesses to build a clearer picture of the events leading up to the negotiation.
- **Surveillance and Reconnaissance**: Using surveillance tools to monitor the situation in real-time and gather visual and auditory information.
- **Digital Footprint**: Analyzing social media, emails, and other digital communications for insights into the motives and state of mind of the individuals involved.

Risk Assessment and Management

Once intelligence is gathered, a thorough risk assessment is essential. This involves identifying potential threats, evaluating their likelihood and potential impact, and developing strategies to mitigate these risks. Key elements of risk assessment include:

- **Threat Analysis**: Identifying specific threats posed by the individuals or situation, such as the presence of weapons or the potential for violence.
- **Impact Assessment**: Evaluating the potential consequences of different actions, including worst-case scenarios.
- **Mitigation Strategies**: Developing plans to minimize risks, such as evacuation procedures, medical readiness, and tactical interventions if necessary.

Establishing a Negotiation Team

Successful negotiations require a coordinated effort from a dedicated team. The composition of the team should include individuals with specialized skills and roles, such as:

- **Primary Negotiator**: The main communicator who interacts directly with the individuals involved.

- **Secondary Negotiator**: Assists the primary negotiator by monitoring the conversation, suggesting strategies, and providing support.
- **Intelligence Officer**: Responsible for gathering and analyzing information to inform the negotiation strategy.
- **Tactical Advisor**: Provides input on tactical options and ensures the negotiation strategy aligns with overall safety protocols.
- **Psychological Expert**: Offers insights into the psychological state of the individuals involved and advises on effective communication techniques.

Understanding the Situation

Identifying Stakeholders and Their Interests

Understanding who is involved and what they want is crucial for effective negotiation. Stakeholders in a negotiation can include:

- **Primary Subjects**: The individuals directly involved in the crisis or conflict.
- **Hostages or Victims**: Individuals who are directly affected by the situation and whose safety is a priority.
- **Family Members and Friends**: Their involvement can influence the negotiation dynamics, either positively or negatively.
- **Community Members**: Their perceptions and reactions can impact the broader context of the negotiation.

Identifying the interests and motivations of each stakeholder helps negotiators tailor their approach to address specific concerns and leverage points.

Analyzing the Environment and Context

The physical and social environment in which the negotiation takes place can significantly impact its dynamics. Key factors to consider include:

- **Location**: The physical setting of the negotiation, including its accessibility, visibility, and any logistical challenges.
- **Time Constraints**: Any deadlines or time pressures that may influence the urgency of the negotiation.
- **Social and Cultural Context**: Understanding the cultural background and social dynamics of the individuals involved to ensure culturally sensitive communication and strategies.

Legal and Ethical Considerations

Negotiators must operate within the boundaries of the law and adhere to ethical standards. Important considerations include:

- **Legal Framework**: Understanding the legal implications of different negotiation tactics and outcomes.
- **Ethical Standards**: Ensuring that all actions taken during the negotiation are ethical, respecting the rights and dignity of all individuals involved.
- **Transparency and Accountability**: Maintaining clear and honest communication with all parties and ensuring that the negotiation process is transparent and accountable.

Developing a Negotiation Strategy

Setting Objectives and Priorities

Clearly defined objectives and priorities guide the negotiation process. These should be realistic, achievable, and aligned with the overall goal of resolving the situation peacefully. Key objectives might include:

- **Ensuring Safety**: The paramount priority is the safety of all

individuals involved.
- **Building Rapport**: Establishing a connection and trust with the individuals involved.
- **Achieving Compliance**: Persuading the individuals to comply with law enforcement directives without resorting to force.

Creating Contingency Plans

Negotiations are inherently unpredictable, and having contingency plans is essential to respond to changing dynamics. This involves:

- **Scenario Planning**: Anticipating different scenarios and developing responses for each.
- **Flexible Tactics**: Being prepared to adapt strategies and tactics as the situation evolves.
- **Crisis Management**: Having plans in place for potential escalations or unexpected developments.

Balancing Firmness and Flexibility

Negotiators must strike a balance between being firm in their demands and flexible in their approach. This balance helps maintain authority while allowing for creative solutions. Key strategies include:

- **Setting Boundaries**: Clearly defining non-negotiable points and communicating them firmly.
- **Offering Options**: Providing alternatives that meet the interests of both parties, creating opportunities for compromise.
- **Adapting to Feedback**: Being responsive to the information and signals received from the individuals involved, adjusting tactics as necessary.

CHAPTER 2

Role-Playing and Simulation Exercises

Importance of Training and Practice

Training and practice are vital for developing and refining negotiation skills. Role-playing and simulation exercises provide realistic scenarios for negotiators to practice their techniques, test strategies, and build confidence. Benefits of training include:

- **Skill Development**: Enhancing communication, active listening, and problem-solving skills.
- **Experience**: Gaining practical experience in handling diverse and challenging situations.
- **Preparedness**: Building readiness to respond effectively to real-world negotiations.

Designing Effective Role-Play Scenarios

Effective role-play scenarios should be realistic, varied, and challenging. Key elements of designing these scenarios include:

- **Realism**: Creating scenarios that closely mimic real-life situations to provide practical experience.
- **Diversity**: Incorporating a range of scenarios to prepare negotiators for different types of crises and conflicts.
- **Challenge**: Introducing complex and dynamic elements to test the negotiator's ability to adapt and respond under pressure.

Debriefing and Feedback Mechanisms

Debriefing and feedback are essential components of the training process. After each role-play or simulation exercise, a thorough debriefing should be conducted to:

- **Analyze Performance**: Reviewing what went well and identifying areas for improvement.
- **Receive Feedback**: Gathering input from trainers, peers, and observers to gain different perspectives.
- **Refine Skills**: Using feedback to refine techniques and strategies, building on strengths, and addressing weaknesses.

Conclusion

Preparation is the cornerstone of effective negotiation in law enforcement. By gathering comprehensive intelligence, assessing risks, understanding the situation, developing a robust strategy, and engaging in rigorous training, negotiators can enhance their readiness to handle complex and high-stakes negotiations. This chapter has outlined the key elements of preparing for negotiation, providing a foundation for the detailed exploration of negotiation techniques and tactics in the subsequent chapters. By mastering these preparatory steps, law enforcement professionals can approach negotiations with confidence, competence, and a clear focus on achieving peaceful and positive outcomes.

Chapter 3

Chapter 3: Crisis Negotiation

Crisis negotiation is a critical skill in law enforcement, involving high-stakes situations where effective communication can mean the difference between life and death. This chapter delves into the various types of crisis situations, the initial steps to establish communication, specific negotiation techniques, managing stress and emotions, and lessons from notable case studies.

Types of Crisis Situations

Hostage Situations

Hostage situations are among the most challenging and dangerous scenarios police negotiators face. In these cases, individuals are held against their will by a subject who may have various motives, including demands for money, political statements, or personal grievances. The primary objective in these situations is to ensure the safe release of hostages while managing the risk to all involved.

Key elements to consider include:

- **Understanding the Motivations**: Determining why the subject

has taken hostages and what their end goals are.
- **Safety Prioritization**: Ensuring the immediate safety of hostages through careful negotiation and tactical planning.
- **Patience and Time Management**: Using time as a tool to de-escalate the situation and create opportunities for resolution.

Suicidal Individuals

Negotiating with individuals threatening to harm themselves requires a unique set of skills and a compassionate approach. The primary goal is to de-escalate the situation and provide support to prevent the individual from acting on their suicidal thoughts.

Important strategies include:

- **Active Listening and Empathy**: Showing genuine concern and understanding to build rapport and trust.
- **Offering Hope and Alternatives**: Providing reasons for the individual to reconsider their actions and offering immediate support options.
- **Involving Mental Health Professionals**: Collaborating with mental health experts to provide specialized support and intervention.

Barricaded Subjects

Barricaded subjects involve individuals who have isolated themselves, often after committing a crime, and refuse to surrender. These situations can vary widely in their level of threat and complexity.

Critical factors include:

- **Assessing the Threat Level**: Determining whether the subject poses an immediate danger to themselves or others.
- **Establishing Communication**: Initiating dialogue with the subject to understand their demands and state of mind.

- **Strategic Patience**: Allowing time for emotions to settle and for the subject to consider peaceful resolution options.

Active Shooters

Active shooter situations are the most urgent and dynamic crisis scenarios, requiring rapid and decisive action to prevent further loss of life. Negotiation plays a secondary but crucial role once the immediate threat is contained.

Key considerations include:

- **Immediate Response**: Swiftly neutralizing the active threat to protect lives.
- **Secondary Negotiation**: Engaging with the subject if they are contained and still armed, aiming to prevent further violence.
- **Post-Incident Debriefing**: Analyzing the incident to learn and improve future response strategies.

Initial Contact and Communication

Establishing Communication Channels

The first step in any crisis negotiation is establishing communication with the subject. This can be achieved through various means, such as:

- **Direct Phone Lines**: Using dedicated phone lines to initiate and maintain contact.
- **Public Address Systems**: Utilizing loudspeakers or public address systems in situations where direct phone contact is not possible.
- **Mediators**: Engaging family members, friends, or other trusted individuals to facilitate communication.

Building Rapport Quickly

Building rapport is crucial in crisis negotiations, as it establishes a foundation of trust and cooperation. Techniques to build rapport quickly include:

- **Introducing Oneself**: Clearly stating the negotiator's name and role to create a personal connection.
- **Expressing Concern**: Showing genuine concern for the subject's well-being and the situation at hand.
- **Finding Common Ground**: Identifying and discussing shared interests or concerns to foster a connection.

Techniques for Active Listening

Active listening is a fundamental skill in crisis negotiation, involving fully engaging with the subject's words and emotions. Techniques include:

- **Reflecting and Paraphrasing**: Repeating back what the subject has said to show understanding and encourage further communication.
- **Asking Open-Ended Questions**: Encouraging the subject to share more information and elaborate on their thoughts.
- **Acknowledging Emotions**: Validating the subject's feelings to show empathy and build trust.

Crisis Negotiation Techniques

Applying the Behavioral Change Stairway Model (BCSM)

The Behavioral Change Stairway Model (BCSM) is a widely used framework in crisis negotiation, consisting of five stages: Active Listening, Empathy, Rapport, Influence, and Behavioral Change. Each stage builds on the previous one to guide the negotiation process.

- **Active Listening**: The foundation of the model, focusing on understanding the subject's perspective.
- **Empathy**: Demonstrating genuine concern and understanding of the subject's emotions.
- **Rapport**: Building a trusting relationship with the subject.
- **Influence**: Using the established rapport to gently steer the subject towards desired outcomes.
- **Behavioral Change**: Achieving a peaceful resolution through the subject's voluntary compliance.

Using Empathy and Validation

Empathy and validation are crucial components of effective negotiation. Empathy involves putting oneself in the subject's shoes, while validation means acknowledging their feelings and perspectives. These techniques help reduce the subject's emotional intensity and open the door to rational dialogue.

Addressing Demands and Deadlines

Negotiators must skillfully address the subject's demands and deadlines, balancing firmness with flexibility. Key strategies include:

- **Clarifying Demands**: Ensuring a clear understanding of what the subject wants and why.
- **Prioritizing Safety**: Evaluating demands based on their impact on safety and feasibility.
- **Negotiating Terms**: Finding mutually acceptable solutions that meet the subject's needs while maintaining safety and order.

Managing Stress and Emotions

Recognizing Signs of Stress

Recognizing signs of stress in both the subject and the negotiation team is vital for maintaining control and effectiveness. Common signs include:

- **Physical Symptoms**: Increased heart rate, sweating, and trembling.
- **Emotional Reactions**: Anxiety, frustration, and anger.
- **Cognitive Impairment**: Difficulty concentrating, making decisions, and recalling information.

Techniques for Staying Calm

Staying calm under pressure is essential for effective negotiation. Techniques include:

- **Deep Breathing**: Using controlled breathing to reduce physical symptoms of stress.
- **Positive Visualization**: Imagining successful outcomes to maintain a positive mindset.
- **Mindfulness**: Practicing mindfulness to stay focused and present in the moment.

Supporting Team Members

Supporting team members is crucial for maintaining overall effectiveness and morale. Strategies include:

- **Regular Check-Ins**: Monitoring team members' well-being and stress levels.
- **Debriefing Sessions**: Conducting regular debriefing sessions to

discuss challenges and provide mutual support.
- **Encouraging Breaks**: Ensuring team members take breaks to rest and recharge during prolonged negotiations.

Case Studies

Detailed Analysis of Notable Crisis Negotiations

Examining detailed case studies of notable crisis negotiations provides valuable insights and lessons. Some key cases to consider include:

- **The 1993 Waco Siege**: Analyzing the negotiation strategies used during the Waco siege and the lessons learned from the tragic outcome.
- **The 2008 Mumbai Attacks**: Exploring the challenges of negotiating during a multi-location terrorist attack and the importance of coordination and communication.
- **The 2013 Cleveland Kidnapping**: Reviewing the successful negotiation tactics that led to the rescue of three women held captive for a decade.

Lessons Learned and Best Practices

Each case study offers lessons and best practices that can be applied to future negotiations. Key takeaways include:

- **Adaptability**: The importance of being flexible and adaptable to changing dynamics.
- **Preparation**: The critical role of thorough preparation and intelligence gathering.
- **Team Coordination**: The necessity of effective communication and coordination among the negotiation team and other law enforcement units.

Conclusion

Crisis negotiation is a complex and demanding field requiring a deep understanding of human behavior, effective communication skills, and the ability to manage stress and emotions under pressure. By exploring the types of crisis situations, initial contact strategies, specific negotiation techniques, and lessons from real-life cases, law enforcement professionals can enhance their ability to handle high-stakes scenarios with confidence and competence. This chapter provides a foundational understanding of crisis negotiation, setting the stage for further exploration of advanced techniques and tactics in subsequent chapters.

Chapter 4

Chapter 4: Tactical Communication Skills

Effective communication is a cornerstone of successful negotiation in law enforcement. This chapter delves into the critical aspects of tactical communication skills, focusing on verbal and non-verbal communication, active listening, persuasion and influence, de-escalation techniques, and conflict resolution.

Verbal and Non-Verbal Communication

Importance of Tone and Body Language

In negotiation, the words spoken are only a part of the message conveyed. Tone and body language play a significant role in how messages are received and interpreted. A calm, steady tone can help de-escalate tension, while aggressive or impatient tones can exacerbate the situation. Similarly, body language such as eye contact, posture, and gestures can reinforce or undermine verbal messages.

- **Tone**: Maintaining a calm, neutral, and controlled tone can help in building rapport and trust. It signals to the subject that the negotiator is composed and empathetic.

- **Body Language**: Open body language, such as uncrossed arms and leaning slightly forward, indicates openness and attentiveness. Avoiding aggressive postures like pointing or standing too close to the subject is crucial.

Techniques for Effective Verbal Communication

Effective verbal communication involves clarity, brevity, and appropriateness. Techniques include using simple language, repeating key points for emphasis, and asking clarifying questions.

- **Simple Language**: Using clear and straightforward language helps prevent misunderstandings. Avoid jargon and complex terms that the subject might not understand.
- **Repetition**: Reiterating important points ensures that the subject comprehends the critical aspects of the negotiation.
- **Clarifying Questions**: Asking open-ended questions encourages the subject to elaborate and provides more information for the negotiator to work with.

Recognizing and Interpreting Non-Verbal Cues

Non-verbal cues such as facial expressions, gestures, and posture provide significant insights into the subject's emotional state and intentions. Recognizing and accurately interpreting these cues is essential for effective negotiation.

- **Facial Expressions**: Emotions like anger, fear, and confusion can be read from facial expressions. Recognizing these can help tailor the negotiation approach.
- **Gestures**: Hand movements and other gestures can indicate agitation, defensiveness, or openness.
- **Posture**: A relaxed posture may indicate willingness to cooperate,

while a tense posture might suggest resistance or aggression.

Active Listening Skills

Components of Active Listening

Active listening is a critical skill in negotiation, involving fully concentrating, understanding, responding, and remembering what the subject says. The key components include:

- **Paying Attention**: Giving the speaker undivided attention, acknowledging their message, and demonstrating understanding through nodding and verbal affirmations.
- **Withholding Judgment**: Avoiding premature judgments or interruptions, allowing the subject to fully express themselves.
- **Reflecting**: Paraphrasing and summarizing what the subject has said to confirm understanding and encourage further dialogue.
- **Clarifying**: Asking questions to clarify any ambiguities and gain a deeper understanding of the subject's perspective.
- **Summarizing**: Summarizing key points to ensure mutual understanding and agreement.

Barriers to Effective Listening

Several barriers can impede effective listening, including distractions, preconceived notions, emotional reactions, and lack of interest. Overcoming these barriers requires conscious effort and practice.

- **Distractions**: Minimizing environmental distractions and focusing solely on the subject can enhance listening effectiveness.
- **Preconceived Notions**: Approaching each negotiation with an open mind, free from biases and assumptions, allows for more effective communication.

- **Emotional Reactions**: Managing personal emotions and remaining calm and objective, even when faced with hostility or aggression, is crucial.
- **Lack of Interest**: Demonstrating genuine interest and concern for the subject's issues fosters a more open and productive dialogue.

Techniques to Improve Listening Skills

Improving listening skills involves practicing active listening techniques, seeking feedback, and engaging in regular training exercises.

- **Active Listening Practice**: Regularly practicing active listening in various scenarios helps hone this skill.
- **Seeking Feedback**: Asking for feedback from colleagues and mentors on listening effectiveness can provide valuable insights.
- **Training Exercises**: Participating in role-playing and simulation exercises designed to enhance listening skills.

Persuasion and Influence

Principles of Persuasion

Persuasion in negotiation relies on principles such as reciprocity, commitment, social proof, authority, liking, and scarcity. Understanding and applying these principles can significantly enhance the negotiator's ability to influence the subject.

- **Reciprocity**: People are more likely to comply with requests if they feel they owe something in return.
- **Commitment**: Once people commit to something, they are more likely to follow through.
- **Social Proof**: People tend to follow the actions of others, especially in uncertain situations.

- **Authority**: People are more likely to be influenced by those they perceive as knowledgeable and credible.
- **Liking**: People are more easily persuaded by those they like and find similar to themselves.
- **Scarcity**: People value things more highly when they perceive them to be scarce.

Techniques for Influencing Behavior

Effective techniques for influencing behavior include building rapport, using positive reinforcement, and framing requests in a way that highlights benefits to the subject.

- **Building Rapport**: Establishing a positive relationship through empathy and mutual respect.
- **Positive Reinforcement**: Encouraging desired behaviors by acknowledging and rewarding them.
- **Framing Requests**: Presenting requests in a way that aligns with the subject's values and interests, emphasizing benefits and positive outcomes.

Ethical Considerations in Persuasion

Persuasion must be conducted ethically, ensuring that the subject's rights and dignity are respected. Manipulative or coercive tactics can lead to distrust and long-term negative consequences.

- **Respect for Autonomy**: Ensuring the subject feels they have a choice and are not being coerced.
- **Honesty and Transparency**: Being truthful and clear about intentions and potential outcomes.
- **Avoiding Manipulation**: Steering clear of deceitful tactics that exploit the subject's vulnerabilities.

De-Escalation Techniques

Strategies for Calming Agitated Individuals

De-escalation involves reducing the intensity of a conflict or potentially violent situation. Strategies include using calm and reassuring language, maintaining a non-threatening posture, and providing the subject with space and time to calm down.

- **Calm and Reassuring Language**: Using a soothing tone and gentle words to help the subject feel safe and understood.
- **Non-Threatening Posture**: Adopting an open and relaxed posture to reduce perceived threats.
- **Providing Space and Time**: Allowing the subject physical space and time to regain composure.

Role of Empathy and Respect

Empathy and respect are crucial in de-escalation, as they help build trust and show the subject that their feelings and perspectives are acknowledged.

- **Empathy**: Demonstrating understanding and compassion for the subject's situation.
- **Respect**: Treating the subject with dignity and acknowledging their concerns as valid.

Avoiding Common Pitfalls

Common pitfalls in de-escalation include reacting emotionally, making threats, and rushing the process. Avoiding these pitfalls requires self-control, patience, and a strategic approach.

- **Emotional Reactions**: Maintaining composure and avoiding

anger or frustration.
- **Making Threats**: Refraining from issuing threats that can escalate the situation.
- **Rushing the Process**: Allowing the negotiation to unfold at a pace that ensures safety and resolution.

Conflict Resolution

Identifying Sources of Conflict

Understanding the underlying causes of conflict is the first step in resolution. Sources can include miscommunication, unmet needs, personality clashes, and differing values.

- **Miscommunication**: Clarifying misunderstandings and ensuring clear communication.
- **Unmet Needs**: Identifying and addressing the needs and interests of all parties.
- **Personality Clashes**: Recognizing and managing interpersonal dynamics.
- **Differing Values**: Finding common ground and respecting differing perspectives.

Techniques for Resolving Disputes

Effective dispute resolution techniques include mediation, negotiation, and collaborative problem-solving.

- **Mediation**: Facilitating a dialogue between conflicting parties to reach a mutually acceptable solution.
- **Negotiation**: Engaging in direct communication to resolve the conflict through compromise and agreement.
- **Collaborative Problem-Solving**: Working together to identify

solutions that satisfy the interests of all parties involved.

Mediation and Facilitation Skills

Mediation and facilitation require specific skills such as neutrality, active listening, and problem-solving.

- **Neutrality**: Remaining impartial and unbiased while facilitating the resolution process.
- **Active Listening**: Ensuring all parties feel heard and understood.
- **Problem-Solving**: Guiding the parties towards practical and acceptable solutions.

Conclusion

Tactical communication skills are essential for effective negotiation and conflict resolution in law enforcement. By mastering verbal and non-verbal communication, active listening, persuasion and influence, de-escalation techniques, and conflict resolution strategies, negotiators can navigate complex and high-stakes situations more effectively. This chapter provides the foundational knowledge and practical techniques necessary for developing these critical skills.

Chapter 5

Chapter 5: Specialized Negotiation Scenarios

Negotiation in law enforcement is not a one-size-fits-all approach. Different scenarios require tailored strategies and a deep understanding of the unique dynamics involved. This chapter explores specialized negotiation scenarios, including domestic violence situations, mental health crises, terrorism and extremism, organized crime negotiations, and kidnapping and ransom situations. Each section provides detailed strategies and considerations to navigate these complex and high-stakes environments effectively.

Domestic Violence Situations

Unique Challenges and Dynamics

Domestic violence situations are often highly emotional and volatile, involving intimate partners or family members. These scenarios present unique challenges due to the deeply personal nature of the conflicts, the presence of power imbalances, and the potential for immediate physical danger.

- **Emotional Intensity**: Domestic disputes can escalate quickly due

to the emotional and personal stakes involved. Negotiators must manage heightened emotions and maintain a calm demeanor.
- **Power Imbalances**: Understanding the dynamics of control and power within the relationship is crucial. The abuser often exerts significant psychological and physical control over the victim.
- **Immediate Danger**: The risk of immediate harm to the victim or others requires swift and strategic action to ensure safety.

Strategies for Negotiation in Domestic Disputes

Effective strategies in domestic violence negotiations focus on de-escalation, empathy, and ensuring the safety of all parties involved.

- **Building Rapport**: Establishing trust quickly is essential. Demonstrating empathy and understanding can help calm the situation and open lines of communication.
- **Active Listening**: Giving both parties an opportunity to speak and feel heard can reduce tension. It's crucial to listen actively and validate their feelings.
- **Calm and Neutral Stance**: Maintaining a neutral and calm demeanor helps to de-escalate the situation and prevents further agitation.
- **Focus on Safety**: Prioritizing the immediate safety of the victim and any children involved. This may involve removing the abuser from the situation or providing a safe space for the victim.

Ensuring the Safety of All Parties

Safety is the primary concern in domestic violence situations. Negotiators must balance the need for immediate intervention with the goal of de-escalation.

- **Immediate Intervention**: If there is an immediate threat to safety,

negotiators must act quickly to neutralize the danger.
- **Safety Planning**: Developing a safety plan for the victim, which may include shelter options, legal resources, and ongoing support.
- **Legal Considerations**: Understanding the legal frameworks and protective measures available, such as restraining orders and emergency custody arrangements.

Mental Health Crises

Understanding Mental Health Issues

Mental health crises can involve individuals experiencing severe distress, psychosis, or suicidal ideation. Negotiators must have a basic understanding of common mental health conditions and the behaviors associated with them.

- **Common Conditions**: Conditions such as schizophrenia, bipolar disorder, and severe depression can impact a person's behavior and decision-making.
- **Behavioral Indicators**: Recognizing signs of mental health crises, such as disorganized thinking, hallucinations, extreme mood swings, and withdrawal from reality.

Techniques for Engaging with Individuals in Crisis

Engaging effectively with individuals in mental health crises requires patience, empathy, and specialized communication techniques.

- **Empathy and Validation**: Demonstrating genuine empathy and validating the person's feelings can help build trust and rapport.
- **Calm Communication**: Speaking slowly, using simple language, and maintaining a calm tone can help soothe an agitated individual.
- **Non-Threatening Approach**: Avoiding sudden movements or

aggressive postures, and giving the individual space to feel less threatened.

Collaborating with Mental Health Professionals
Involving mental health professionals can provide valuable insights and support in managing mental health crises.

- **Multidisciplinary Approach**: Working closely with mental health professionals, social workers, and crisis intervention teams to develop a comprehensive response plan.
- **Training and Education**: Ensuring that negotiators receive ongoing training in mental health awareness and crisis intervention techniques.
- **Resource Coordination**: Coordinating with mental health facilities and community resources to provide appropriate follow-up care and support.

Terrorism and Extremism

Specific Challenges in Negotiating with Terrorists
Negotiating with terrorists presents unique challenges due to their often rigid ideological beliefs, willingness to use extreme violence, and complex organizational structures.

- **Ideological Rigidity**: Terrorists may have non-negotiable demands based on ideological or religious beliefs, making compromise difficult.
- **Violence and Coercion**: The threat or use of extreme violence to achieve their goals can escalate the stakes of the negotiation.
- **Organizational Complexity**: Understanding the hierarchy and decision-making processes within terrorist organizations is critical

for effective negotiation.

Strategies for Hostage Negotiations Involving Terrorists

Hostage negotiations with terrorists require a strategic approach that balances communication with tactical readiness.

- **Establishing Communication**: Opening lines of communication is the first step. This involves identifying a spokesperson and maintaining a dialogue.
- **Building Trust**: Developing a level of trust and rapport, despite the adversarial nature of the situation, can facilitate negotiation.
- **Tactical Readiness**: Being prepared for tactical intervention if negotiations fail. This includes having a clear operational plan and coordination with tactical teams.

Balancing Negotiation and Tactical Intervention

Finding the right balance between negotiation and the potential need for tactical intervention is crucial in terrorism-related scenarios.

- **Risk Assessment**: Continuously assessing the risk to hostages and the broader public to determine the appropriate course of action.
- **Decision Points**: Establishing clear decision points for when to transition from negotiation to tactical intervention.
- **Coordination**: Ensuring seamless communication and coordination between negotiators and tactical units.

Negotiating with Organized Crime

Understanding the Structure and Behavior of Criminal Organizations

Negotiating with organized crime involves understanding the hierarchical structure, codes of conduct, and motivations of criminal organizations.

- **Hierarchy and Roles**: Recognizing the roles and influence of different members within the organization.
- **Codes of Conduct**: Understanding the unwritten rules and codes that govern behavior within the organization.
- **Motivations**: Identifying the motivations and interests driving the organization's actions, such as financial gain, power, or territory.

Strategies for Effective Negotiation

Effective strategies for negotiating with organized crime focus on leveraging information, building alliances, and maintaining a strong legal and ethical stance.

- **Information Leverage**: Using intelligence and information about the organization to gain leverage in negotiations.
- **Building Alliances**: Identifying and collaborating with potential allies within the organization who may be more amenable to negotiation.
- **Legal and Ethical Stance**: Ensuring that all negotiation tactics are legally sound and ethically justifiable.

Legal and Ethical Considerations

Negotiating with organized crime requires adherence to strict legal and ethical standards to avoid complicity or corruption.

- **Legal Compliance**: Ensuring all actions and agreements comply with local, national, and international laws.
- **Ethical Integrity**: Maintaining ethical integrity and transparency throughout the negotiation process to uphold public trust.

CHAPTER 5

Kidnapping and Ransom Situations

Dynamics of Kidnapping Situations

Kidnapping situations involve complex dynamics, including the motivations of the kidnappers, the condition and treatment of the hostages, and the involvement of multiple stakeholders.

- **Motivations**: Understanding whether the kidnapping is financially motivated, politically driven, or for personal revenge.
- **Hostage Condition**: Monitoring the health and safety of the hostages and maintaining communication to ensure their well-being.
- **Stakeholder Involvement**: Coordinating with families, employers, and possibly international agencies, depending on the context of the kidnapping.

Negotiation Strategies and Tactics

Effective negotiation in kidnapping and ransom situations involves a careful balance of communication, patience, and strategic pressure.

- **Initial Contact**: Establishing communication with the kidnappers and ensuring they understand the willingness to negotiate.
- **Building Rapport**: Developing a rapport with the kidnappers to facilitate negotiation and ensure the hostages' safety.
- **Strategic Patience**: Exercising patience and avoiding rash decisions, while applying strategic pressure to achieve a resolution.

Working with Families and Other Stakeholders

Families and other stakeholders play a critical role in kidnapping negotiations. Managing their expectations and emotions is crucial for a successful outcome.

- **Family Support**: Providing emotional support and clear communication to the families of hostages.
- **Stakeholder Coordination**: Ensuring all stakeholders are informed and involved in the negotiation process.
- **Media Management**: Managing media involvement to prevent interference with the negotiation process and protect the privacy of the hostages and their families.

Conclusion

Specialized negotiation scenarios require tailored strategies and a deep understanding of the unique dynamics involved. Whether dealing with domestic violence, mental health crises, terrorism, organized crime, or kidnapping, negotiators must apply specific techniques and principles to navigate these complex situations effectively. This chapter provides detailed guidance on handling these high-stakes scenarios, emphasizing the importance of safety, empathy, strategic planning, and collaboration. By mastering these specialized negotiation skills, law enforcement professionals can enhance their ability to resolve crises and protect the well-being of all parties involved.

Chapter 6

Chapter 6: Building and Leading a Negotiation Team

Effective negotiation in law enforcement requires a well-structured, cohesive, and highly trained team. Building and leading such a team involves understanding key roles, fostering strong leadership, ensuring continuous training, and coordinating with other units and agencies. This chapter explores the intricacies of forming and managing a negotiation team, providing detailed insights into the essential components and strategies for success.

Team Structure and Roles

Key Roles in a Negotiation Team

A successful negotiation team comprises various roles, each critical to the operation's overall success. Understanding these roles and their responsibilities is fundamental to building an effective team.

- **Primary Negotiator:** The face of the negotiation, responsible for direct communication with the subject. This individual needs exceptional communication and psychological skills to manage the

dialogue effectively.
- **Secondary Negotiator**: Also known as the coach, this team member supports the primary negotiator, offering advice, monitoring the conversation, and ensuring the negotiation strategy is followed.
- **Intelligence Officer**: Gathers and analyzes information about the subject, situation, and environment. This role is crucial for making informed decisions during the negotiation.
- **Team Leader**: Oversees the entire negotiation team, making strategic decisions and ensuring that all team members are functioning effectively and cohesively.
- **Mental Health Professional**: Provides psychological insights and strategies, particularly useful in situations involving individuals with mental health issues.

Responsibilities and Expectations

Each team member has specific responsibilities and expectations that contribute to the team's overall effectiveness.

- **Primary Negotiator**: Establish rapport, engage in active listening, and manage the flow of communication with the subject. They must stay calm under pressure and adapt to changing situations.
- **Secondary Negotiator**: Monitor the negotiation process, offer real-time feedback, and help adjust tactics as needed. This role requires strong analytical and supportive skills.
- **Intelligence Officer**: Continuously gather and assess information, liaise with other agencies, and provide the negotiation team with up-to-date intelligence.
- **Team Leader**: Coordinate team efforts, make critical decisions, and manage the overall strategy. Strong leadership and decision-making skills are essential.
- **Mental Health Professional**: Assess the psychological state of the

subject, advise on communication strategies, and support the team in managing stress and emotional challenges.

Selecting Team Members

Choosing the right team members is crucial. Candidates should possess specific skills and characteristics that make them suitable for their roles.

- **Communication Skills**: Essential for negotiators who need to manage dialogue and build rapport.
- **Analytical Abilities**: Important for intelligence officers who must assess information accurately and quickly.
- **Emotional Stability**: All team members should be able to remain calm and focused under pressure.
- **Training and Experience**: Prior training in negotiation techniques and relevant experience in similar scenarios enhance a team member's effectiveness.

Leadership and Team Dynamics

Effective Leadership Skills

Leadership in a negotiation team involves guiding, supporting, and motivating team members to achieve common goals. Key leadership skills include:

- **Decision-Making**: Ability to make informed, timely decisions under pressure.
- **Communication**: Clear and concise communication with team members and other units.
- **Empathy**: Understanding and addressing the needs and concerns of team members.

- **Adaptability**: Flexibility to adjust strategies and tactics as situations evolve.

Managing Team Dynamics and Conflict

Effective team management involves understanding and navigating the dynamics and potential conflicts within the team.

- **Building Trust**: Fostering an environment of trust and mutual respect among team members.
- **Conflict Resolution**: Addressing and resolving conflicts quickly and fairly to maintain team cohesion.
- **Encouraging Collaboration**: Promoting a collaborative approach where team members share ideas and support each other.

Ensuring Effective Communication Within the Team

Clear and consistent communication is vital for a negotiation team to function effectively.

- **Regular Briefings**: Conducting regular briefings to keep everyone informed about the situation and strategy.
- **Open Feedback Channels**: Encouraging open feedback and discussion to refine tactics and address concerns.
- **Technology Utilization**: Using communication tools and technology to facilitate real-time information sharing and coordination.

Training and Development

Ongoing Training Programs

Continuous training ensures that team members are up-to-date with the latest negotiation techniques and strategies.

- **Skill Development**: Regular training sessions focusing on communication, psychological principles, and tactical strategies.
- **Scenario-Based Training**: Using real-life scenarios to practice and refine negotiation skills.
- **Interdisciplinary Training**: Collaborating with mental health professionals, tactical units, and other experts to broaden the team's knowledge and capabilities.

Importance of Simulations and Drills

Simulations and drills are critical components of training, providing practical experience in a controlled environment.

- **Realistic Scenarios**: Designing simulations that mimic real-life situations to test and improve team performance.
- **Role-Playing**: Engaging in role-playing exercises to practice different negotiation tactics and strategies.
- **Debriefing**: Conducting thorough debriefs after each simulation to discuss what went well, identify areas for improvement, and implement lessons learned.

Continuous Learning and Improvement

A commitment to continuous learning and improvement is essential for maintaining a high-performing negotiation team.

- **Feedback Loops**: Establishing mechanisms for continuous feedback and improvement.
- **Professional Development**: Encouraging team members to pursue additional training, certifications, and education.
- **Staying Updated**: Keeping abreast of the latest research, techniques, and best practices in negotiation and crisis management.

Coordination with Other Units

Working with Tactical Units

Effective coordination with tactical units is crucial, particularly in high-stakes situations where the potential for violence is high.

- **Joint Planning**: Collaborating on the development of negotiation and tactical plans to ensure seamless integration.
- **Communication Protocols**: Establishing clear communication protocols to maintain coordination and information flow.
- **Shared Objectives**: Ensuring that both negotiation and tactical units have a shared understanding of the objectives and strategies.

Collaboration with External Agencies

Collaboration with external agencies, such as mental health services, social services, and other law enforcement agencies, enhances the negotiation team's capabilities.

- **Interagency Cooperation**: Building relationships and protocols for working with external agencies.
- **Resource Sharing**: Leveraging the resources and expertise of external agencies to support negotiation efforts.
- **Joint Training**: Participating in joint training exercises to improve coordination and understanding between agencies.

Integrating Negotiation and Tactical Plans

Integrating negotiation and tactical plans ensures that both approaches complement each other and contribute to the overall strategy.

- **Unified Strategy**: Developing a unified strategy that incorporates both negotiation and tactical elements.

- **Flexible Plans**: Creating flexible plans that can adapt to changing circumstances and new information.
- **Clear Roles**: Defining clear roles and responsibilities for both negotiation and tactical teams to avoid confusion and overlap.

Conclusion

Building and leading a negotiation team requires a strategic approach that encompasses team structure, leadership, training, and coordination with other units. By understanding the key roles and responsibilities, fostering effective leadership, ensuring continuous training, and collaborating with tactical units and external agencies, law enforcement professionals can create a high-performing negotiation team capable of handling complex and high-stakes situations. This chapter provides a comprehensive guide to building and managing a successful negotiation team, emphasizing the importance of preparation, communication, and continuous improvement.

Chapter 7

Chapter 7: Technological Tools in Negotiation

In the evolving landscape of law enforcement, technology has become an indispensable ally in negotiation processes. This chapter delves into the critical role that technological tools play in enhancing negotiation strategies and outcomes. We will explore the various communication technologies, surveillance and intelligence-gathering methods, data analysis tools, and emerging innovations that are reshaping the field of police negotiation.

Communication Technology

Effective communication is the bedrock of successful negotiations. The ability to maintain clear, secure, and reliable communication channels can significantly influence the outcome of a negotiation scenario.

Radios, Phones, and Other Communication Devices

Radios and phones are fundamental tools for any negotiation team. Radios provide instant communication among team members, allowing for swift coordination and response. They are particularly useful in dynamic situations where immediate updates and instructions are crucial. Modern radios come equipped with features such as encrypted channels, GPS tracking, and long-range capabilities, making them highly versatile.

Phones, both mobile and satellite, are essential for direct communication with subjects. In hostage or barricade situations, establishing a line of communication with the suspect is a critical first step. Phones allow negotiators to initiate contact, build rapport, and engage in meaningful dialogue. Satellite phones are especially valuable in remote areas where conventional mobile networks may not be available.

Secure Communication Channels

Security is paramount in negotiation communications to prevent unauthorized access and ensure the integrity of sensitive information. Encryption technologies play a crucial role in securing voice and data transmissions, making it difficult for third parties to intercept or decipher the communications.

Dedicated communication networks, such as those provided by specialized law enforcement communication systems, offer additional layers of security. These networks are designed to function reliably even in challenging environments and provide a secure platform for transmitting critical information.

Redundancy is another important aspect of secure communication. Having backup communication systems ensures that the negotiation team can maintain contact even if the primary system fails. This redundancy is achieved through the use of multiple communication devices and networks, including radios, mobile phones, and satellite phones.

Overcoming Technological Challenges

Despite the advantages, technological tools can present challenges that need to be addressed proactively. Interference from physical barriers, weather conditions, or deliberate jamming can disrupt communication signals. Using signal boosters, selecting appropriate frequencies, and having alternative communication methods can help mitigate these issues.

Technical failures, such as equipment malfunctions, are another potential challenge. Regular maintenance, thorough testing before deployment, and having spare equipment on hand can prevent such issues from compromising the negotiation process.

Training is also critical. All team members must be proficient in using the available technological tools. Regular training sessions, simulations, and drills can help ensure that everyone is comfortable and effective in using the equipment under various conditions.

Surveillance and Intelligence Gathering

Accurate and timely information is crucial for informed decision-making during negotiations. Surveillance and intelligence-gathering tools provide the data needed to understand the situation and develop effective strategies.

Tools for Gathering Real-Time Information

Drones, cameras, and audio surveillance devices are among the most effective tools for gathering real-time information.

- **Drones**: Drones provide an aerial perspective, offering valuable insights into the layout of the area, the positions of suspects

and hostages, and potential escape routes. Equipped with high-resolution cameras and thermal imaging, drones can operate in various conditions, including low light and adverse weather.
- **Cameras**: Fixed and mobile cameras allow continuous monitoring of key areas. Body-worn cameras provide real-time footage from the perspective of officers on the ground, adding another layer of situational awareness.
- **Audio Surveillance**: Directional microphones and other audio devices can capture conversations and other sounds from a distance, providing insights into the suspect's state of mind and intentions.

Using Drones, Cameras, and Other Surveillance Methods

Effective deployment of surveillance tools requires careful planning and execution. Drones should be used to monitor areas that are difficult or dangerous for personnel to access. Strategic placement of fixed cameras can cover entry and exit points, while mobile cameras can provide dynamic coverage as the situation evolves.

Audio surveillance devices should be positioned where they can capture relevant sounds without being detected by the suspects. It is crucial to balance the need for information with respect for privacy and legal considerations.

Ethical Considerations in Surveillance

Surveillance must be conducted ethically and legally to maintain public trust and protect individual rights. Privacy concerns should be addressed by ensuring that surveillance activities are justified, proportionate, and conducted within the bounds of the law.

Transparency about the use of surveillance tools and adherence to established protocols can help build public confidence. Regular reviews and audits of surveillance practices can ensure compliance with ethical standards and legal requirements.

Data Analysis and Decision Support

Incorporating data analysis into negotiation strategies can significantly enhance decision-making. Advanced analytical tools provide valuable insights and support informed decisions.

Utilizing Data for Strategic Decisions

Data from various sources, including surveillance footage, communication logs, and historical records, can be analyzed to identify patterns and trends. This information helps negotiators understand the behavior of suspects, anticipate their actions, and develop effective strategies.

Tools for Analyzing Negotiation Scenarios

Specialized software tools can simulate different negotiation scenarios, allowing teams to explore various strategies and their potential outcomes. These tools can model the behavior of suspects based on psychological principles and historical data, providing a deeper understanding of the situation.

Predictive analytics can forecast the likely responses of suspects to different negotiation tactics. By analyzing large datasets, these tools can identify factors that influence the success of negotiations and recommend the most effective approaches.

Predictive Analytics in Negotiation

Predictive analytics involves using statistical algorithms and machine learning techniques to predict future events based on historical data. In negotiations, predictive analytics can identify key factors that contribute to successful outcomes, such as the timing of concessions, the use of specific communication techniques, and the impact of external influences.

By leveraging predictive analytics, negotiation teams can make more informed decisions and increase their chances of achieving favorable outcomes. These tools can also help identify potential risks and develop contingency plans to address them.

Technological Innovations

The field of negotiation is continually evolving, with new technologies emerging that offer additional capabilities and insights.

Emerging Technologies in Negotiation

Several emerging technologies hold promise for enhancing negotiation strategies. Virtual reality (VR) and augmented reality (AR) can create immersive training environments that simulate real-life negotiation scenarios. These technologies allow negotiators to practice their skills in a safe and controlled setting, improving their readiness for actual situations.

Artificial intelligence (AI) is another area with significant potential. AI algorithms can analyze vast amounts of data to identify patterns and trends, providing insights that human analysts might miss. AI-powered tools can assist with real-time decision-making, offering recommendations based on the latest data and predictive models.

Future Trends and Developments

As technology continues to advance, new tools and capabilities will emerge that further enhance negotiation strategies. The integration of AI, machine learning, and big data analytics will provide deeper insights and more accurate predictions.

Advancements in communication technologies, such as 5G networks, will enable faster and more reliable data transmission, improving coordination and response times. Innovations in surveillance technologies, such as improved sensor capabilities and autonomous drones, will enhance situational awareness and intelligence gathering.

Impact of Technology on Negotiation Strategies

The integration of advanced technologies into negotiation strategies will fundamentally change how negotiations are conducted. These tools will provide negotiators with more information, better insights, and more effective communication channels, allowing for more precise and informed decision-making.

However, it is important to balance the use of technology with human judgment and expertise. While technology can enhance capabilities, the core principles of negotiation—such as empathy, rapport building, and ethical considerations—remain essential.

In conclusion, technological tools play a critical role in modern police negotiations. By leveraging communication technologies, surveillance and intelligence-gathering tools, data analysis, and emerging innovations, negotiation teams can improve their effectiveness and achieve better outcomes. As technology continues to evolve, staying informed about the latest developments and integrating them into negotiation strategies will be crucial for law enforcement agencies.

Chapter 8

Chapter 8: Ethical and Legal Considerations

In the realm of police negotiation, adherence to ethical and legal standards is paramount. Negotiators must navigate complex situations while upholding the law and maintaining the highest ethical standards. This chapter explores the legal frameworks, ethical principles, accountability measures, and cultural sensitivities that guide police negotiations.

Legal Framework for Negotiation

Understanding the legal framework that governs police negotiations is crucial for ensuring that all actions taken are within the bounds of the law. This involves knowledge of relevant laws, the rights of suspects and hostages, and adherence to legal standards.

Relevant Laws and Regulations

Police negotiators must be well-versed in the legal statutes and regulations that pertain to their actions. These include:

- **Constitutional Rights**: Understanding the constitutional rights of suspects and hostages, such as the right to due process, protection against unreasonable searches and seizures, and the right to counsel.
- **Criminal Law**: Familiarity with criminal statutes that define illegal activities and the penalties associated with them. This knowledge helps negotiators understand the legal implications of the suspect's actions.
- **Hostage and Barricade Laws**: Specific laws and protocols that apply to hostage and barricade situations, including the permissible actions of law enforcement and the rights of the individuals involved.
- **Use of Force Regulations**: Guidelines on the use of force, which dictate when and how force can be applied, ensuring it is proportional, necessary, and within legal boundaries.

Legal Rights of Suspects and Hostages

Respecting the legal rights of all parties involved in a negotiation is fundamental. This includes:

- **Suspect Rights**: Ensuring that suspects are aware of their rights, such as the right to remain silent, the right to an attorney, and protection against self-incrimination.
- **Hostage Rights**: Protecting the rights and well-being of hostages, including their right to safety and humane treatment.
- **Due Process**: Adhering to due process principles to ensure that all actions taken during the negotiation are fair and lawful.

CHAPTER 8

Ensuring Compliance with Legal Standards

Compliance with legal standards involves:

- **Documentation**: Keeping detailed records of all negotiation activities, decisions, and communications. This documentation serves as evidence of adherence to legal standards.
- **Training**: Regular training for negotiators on legal updates and best practices to ensure they are equipped with the latest legal knowledge.
- **Oversight**: Establishing oversight mechanisms to review negotiation processes and outcomes, ensuring they align with legal requirements.

Ethical Principles in Negotiation

Ethical considerations are integral to the conduct of police negotiations. Negotiators must balance operational needs with ethical principles, often facing challenging dilemmas.

Balancing Ethical Considerations with Operational Needs

Negotiators must make decisions that align with ethical principles while achieving operational objectives. This balance involves:

- **Respect for Human Dignity**: Treating all individuals with respect and dignity, regardless of their actions or status.
- **Integrity and Honesty**: Maintaining honesty in all communications and actions, avoiding deception unless absolutely necessary and ethically justifiable.
- **Responsibility**: Taking responsibility for the outcomes of negoti-

ation decisions and actions, and striving to minimize harm.

Common Ethical Dilemmas in Negotiation

Negotiators often encounter ethical dilemmas, such as:

- **Deception vs. Honesty**: Deciding when, if ever, to use deception to gain a tactical advantage without compromising ethical standards.
- **Use of Force**: Balancing the need to use force to protect lives with the ethical obligation to minimize harm.
- **Privacy vs. Surveillance**: Weighing the need for surveillance to gather critical information against the right to privacy of individuals.

Strategies for Ethical Decision-Making

Ethical decision-making strategies include:

- **Ethical Training**: Providing negotiators with training on ethical principles and decision-making frameworks.
- **Consultation**: Encouraging negotiators to consult with peers, supervisors, and legal advisors when faced with ethical dilemmas.
- **Reflective Practice**: Promoting reflective practices where negotiators review their decisions and actions to learn and improve their ethical conduct.

Accountability and Transparency

Accountability and transparency are essential for maintaining public trust and ensuring the integrity of the negotiation process.

Importance of Accountability in Negotiations

Accountability involves:

- **Responsibility for Actions**: Negotiators must be accountable for their actions and decisions, ensuring they are justifiable and lawful.
- **Performance Reviews**: Regular performance reviews and evaluations of negotiators to ensure they adhere to ethical and legal standards.

Documenting and Reviewing Negotiation Processes

Thorough documentation and review processes include:

- **Detailed Records**: Keeping comprehensive records of all negotiations, including communications, decisions, and outcomes.
- **After-Action Reviews**: Conducting after-action reviews to evaluate the negotiation process, identify lessons learned, and make necessary improvements.

Ensuring Transparency with Stakeholders

Transparency involves:

- **Public Communication**: Providing clear and accurate information to the public and media about negotiation processes and

outcomes, within the bounds of operational security.
- **Stakeholder Involvement**: Engaging with stakeholders, including community leaders, legal advisors, and oversight bodies, to ensure transparency and accountability.

Cultural Sensitivity and Diversity

Cultural sensitivity and diversity are crucial in negotiations, particularly in diverse and multicultural societies. Understanding and respecting cultural differences can enhance the effectiveness of negotiations.

Understanding Cultural Differences in Negotiation

Cultural differences can significantly impact negotiation dynamics. Understanding these differences involves:

- **Cultural Awareness**: Recognizing and respecting cultural norms, values, and communication styles of the individuals involved in the negotiation.
- **Bias and Stereotyping**: Being aware of and addressing any biases or stereotypes that may affect the negotiation process.

Strategies for Negotiating Across Cultures

Effective strategies for negotiating across cultures include:

- **Cultural Training**: Providing negotiators with training on cultural competence and sensitivity.
- **Interpreters and Cultural Advisors**: Utilizing interpreters and cultural advisors to bridge communication gaps and provide cultural insights.

- **Building Rapport**: Developing rapport and trust with individuals from different cultural backgrounds through respectful and culturally appropriate interactions.

Promoting Diversity within the Negotiation Team

Diversity within the negotiation team enhances its effectiveness by bringing different perspectives and insights. Promoting diversity involves:

- **Inclusive Recruitment**: Recruiting negotiators from diverse backgrounds to reflect the community they serve.
- **Diverse Leadership**: Ensuring diversity in leadership positions within the negotiation team.
- **Cultural Competence Training**: Providing ongoing training on cultural competence and diversity to all team members.

In conclusion, ethical and legal considerations are fundamental to the practice of police negotiation. By adhering to legal frameworks, upholding ethical principles, ensuring accountability and transparency, and promoting cultural sensitivity and diversity, negotiators can conduct their work with integrity and effectiveness. These principles not only enhance the success of negotiations but also build public trust and confidence in law enforcement agencies.

Chapter 9

Chapter 9: Post-Negotiation Analysis

Effective negotiation doesn't end when the immediate crisis is resolved; rather, it extends into a critical phase of post-negotiation analysis. This chapter explores the importance of debriefing and evaluation, learning from both successes and failures, addressing the psychological impact on negotiators, and creating a robust knowledge base. Through detailed post-negotiation analysis, law enforcement agencies can continuously improve their tactics, strategies, and overall effectiveness in handling future crises.

Debriefing and Evaluation

Importance of Post-Negotiation Debriefing

Post-negotiation debriefing is a crucial step that ensures comprehensive reflection on the negotiation process. This phase provides an opportunity to analyze what transpired, understand decision-making dynamics, and gather insights for future operations. Effective debriefing helps:

- **Identify Strengths and Weaknesses**: Recognize what worked

well and areas that need improvement.
- **Accountability**: Ensure that all actions taken are reviewed and accountable.
- **Emotional Closure**: Provide negotiators and team members with emotional closure after high-stress situations.

Techniques for Effective Debriefing

Effective debriefing requires structured techniques to maximize the benefits of this process. These include:

- **Structured Format**: Use a standardized format for debriefing sessions, covering all critical aspects of the negotiation.
- **Open Discussion**: Encourage open and honest discussions where all team members can share their perspectives.
- **Facilitator Role**: Use a skilled facilitator to guide the debriefing process, ensuring it remains focused and productive.
- **Documentation**: Document all key points discussed during the debriefing for future reference and training purposes.

Evaluating Performance and Outcomes

Performance evaluation is integral to understanding the effectiveness of the negotiation. This involves:

- **Metrics and Criteria**: Establishing clear metrics and criteria for evaluating the success of the negotiation.
- **Outcome Analysis**: Assessing the outcomes against the initial objectives and goals.
- **Feedback Mechanisms**: Implementing mechanisms for receiving feedback from all involved parties, including negotiators, tactical

teams, and external stakeholders.

Learning from Successes and Failures

Analyzing Successful Negotiations

Successful negotiations provide valuable insights and lessons that can be applied to future scenarios. Analysis of successful cases involves:

- **Case Study Development**: Creating detailed case studies that document the negotiation process, strategies used, and factors contributing to success.
- **Best Practices**: Identifying best practices and effective techniques that can be standardized across the negotiation team.
- **Recognition and Reward**: Recognizing and rewarding team members for their successful efforts, which can boost morale and encourage continuous improvement.

Learning from Unsuccessful Negotiations

Unsuccessful negotiations, while challenging, offer critical learning opportunities. This analysis involves:

- **Root Cause Analysis**: Conducting a thorough analysis to identify the root causes of failure.
- **Identifying Mistakes**: Recognizing and understanding mistakes made during the negotiation to avoid them in the future.
- **Developing Mitigation Strategies**: Creating strategies to mitigate similar risks and challenges in future negotiations.
- **Constructive Criticism**: Providing constructive feedback to team members, focusing on improvement rather than blame.

Continuous Improvement Strategies

Continuous improvement is key to maintaining and enhancing negotiation capabilities. Strategies include:

- **Regular Training**: Incorporating lessons learned into regular training and development programs.
- **Process Refinement**: Continuously refining negotiation processes and protocols based on post-negotiation analysis.
- **Innovation and Adaptation**: Encouraging innovation and adaptation of new techniques and technologies to improve negotiation outcomes.

Psychological Impact on Negotiators

Recognizing Signs of Stress and Burnout

Negotiation, especially in high-stress and high-stakes situations, can have a significant psychological impact on negotiators. Recognizing signs of stress and burnout is crucial:

- **Symptoms of Stress**: Identifying symptoms such as fatigue, irritability, anxiety, and difficulty concentrating.
- **Burnout Indicators**: Recognizing indicators of burnout, including emotional exhaustion, cynicism, and reduced performance.

Providing Psychological Support

Providing psychological support to negotiators is essential for maintaining their well-being and effectiveness. This includes:

- **Access to Mental Health Professionals**: Ensuring negotiators have access to mental health professionals for counseling and support.
- **Peer Support Programs**: Implementing peer support programs where negotiators can share experiences and support each other.
- **Stress Management Training**: Offering training on stress management techniques and resilience building.

Building Resilience in Negotiation Teams

Building resilience within negotiation teams helps them cope with the demands of their role. Strategies include:

- **Resilience Training**: Providing training programs focused on building psychological resilience.
- **Team Building Activities**: Conducting team-building activities to strengthen camaraderie and mutual support.
- **Regular Check-ins**: Implementing regular check-ins with team members to monitor their well-being and address any concerns.

Creating a Knowledge Base

Documenting Best Practices

Documenting best practices from negotiations is vital for preserving institutional knowledge and improving future performance:

- **Standard Operating Procedures (SOPs)**: Developing SOPs based on best practices identified through post-negotiation analysis.
- **Guidelines and Manuals**: Creating comprehensive guidelines and manuals for negotiators, incorporating best practices and lessons

learned.

Creating Case Study Repositories

Case study repositories serve as valuable resources for training and development:

- **Comprehensive Case Studies**: Developing detailed case studies that cover various aspects of the negotiation process.
- **Accessible Repositories**: Ensuring these case studies are easily accessible to all team members for reference and learning.

Sharing Knowledge within the Law Enforcement Community

Sharing knowledge within the broader law enforcement community enhances collective capabilities:

- **Inter-agency Collaboration**: Promoting collaboration and knowledge sharing between different law enforcement agencies.
- **Workshops and Seminars**: Organizing workshops, seminars, and conferences to disseminate knowledge and best practices.
- **Publications and Journals**: Contributing to professional publications and journals to share insights and developments in negotiation techniques.

In conclusion, post-negotiation analysis is a critical phase that encompasses debriefing, learning from successes and failures, addressing the psychological impact on negotiators, and creating a comprehensive knowledge base. By systematically analyzing each negotiation and incorporating lessons learned into ongoing training and development, law enforcement agencies can continuously improve their negotiation capabilities, ensuring better outcomes and the well-being of their personnel. This commitment to reflection, learning, and growth is essential for maintaining the highest standards of professionalism and effectiveness in police negotiation.

Chapter 10

Chapter 10: Conclusion

Summary of Key Points

As we conclude this comprehensive guide on police negotiation methods and tactics, it is essential to reflect on the major themes and lessons presented throughout the book. Each chapter has contributed to building a robust understanding of negotiation in law enforcement, emphasizing the importance of preparation, communication, psychological insight, and technological integration.

Fundamentals of Police Negotiation: We began with the fundamentals, defining police negotiation and highlighting its critical role in modern policing. Effective negotiation is not just about resolving conflicts but also about building trust, de-escalating potentially violent situations, and minimizing the use of force.

Preparing for Negotiation: Preparation is paramount. From gathering intelligence and conducting risk assessments to developing negotiation strategies and engaging in role-playing exercises, thorough preparation sets the stage for successful outcomes. Understanding the context, identifying stakeholders, and planning for various scenarios are crucial steps.

Crisis Negotiation: We explored the nuances of crisis negotiation, addressing various high-stress situations such as hostage scenarios, suicidal individuals, barricaded subjects, and active shooters. Techniques for establishing initial contact, building rapport, and managing stress were discussed, underscoring the importance of empathy and calm communication.

Tactical Communication Skills: Communication is at the heart of negotiation. We delved into the significance of verbal and non-verbal communication, active listening, persuasion, and de-escalation techniques. These skills are vital for negotiators to influence behavior, resolve conflicts, and achieve peaceful resolutions.

Specialized Negotiation Scenarios: Each specialized scenario, from domestic violence and mental health crises to terrorism, extremism, organized crime, and kidnapping, presents unique challenges. We examined tailored strategies for each, emphasizing the need for flexibility, cultural sensitivity, and collaboration with other professionals and agencies.

Building and Leading a Negotiation Team: Effective negotiation requires a well-structured and cohesive team. We discussed the importance of defining roles, leadership skills, training, and maintaining team dynamics. Coordination with other units and agencies enhances the overall effectiveness of negotiation efforts.

Technological Tools in Negotiation: Technology plays an increasingly significant role in modern negotiations. Communication devices, surveillance tools, data analysis, and emerging technologies offer new opportunities for real-time information gathering, strategic decision-making, and enhancing negotiation outcomes.

Ethical and Legal Considerations: Navigating the legal and ethical landscape is critical. We highlighted the legal frameworks governing negotiation, ethical principles, accountability, transparency, and cultural sensitivity. Ethical decision-making ensures that negotiations are conducted with integrity and respect for all parties involved.

Post-Negotiation Analysis: Finally, we emphasized the importance of post-negotiation analysis. Debriefing, learning from successes and failures, addressing the psychological impact on negotiators, and creating a knowledge base contribute to continuous improvement. This reflective practice ensures that each negotiation builds on the lessons of the past, fostering growth and resilience within negotiation teams.

Future Trends in Police Negotiation

As we look to the future, several emerging trends and challenges will shape the landscape of police negotiation:

Technological Advancements: Continued advancements in technology will revolutionize negotiation tactics. Artificial intelligence, machine learning, and predictive analytics will provide deeper insights and enhance decision-making processes. Virtual and augmented reality could transform training and simulation exercises.

Complexity of Threats: The nature of threats is evolving, with increased incidences of cybercrime, terrorism, and organized crime. Negotiators must adapt to these complexities, developing specialized skills and strategies to address new forms of criminal activity.

Mental Health Awareness: There is growing recognition of the importance of mental health in both the individuals involved in negotiations and the negotiators themselves. Greater emphasis on mental health training, support systems, and collaboration with mental health professionals will be essential.

Community Policing and Trust-Building: The role of negotiation in community policing will continue to expand. Building trust within communities, fostering open communication, and involving community leaders in negotiation processes will strengthen relationships and enhance public safety.

Globalization and Cultural Sensitivity: Globalization requires negotiators to be culturally aware and sensitive to diverse backgrounds. Training programs must incorporate cultural competence, and strategies should be adapted to effectively communicate and negotiate across cultures.

Final Thoughts

Effective negotiation is more than a tactical skill; it is an art that requires empathy, patience, and continuous learning. As you conclude this book, take with you the understanding that every negotiation is an opportunity to build bridges, resolve conflicts, and enhance community safety.

To all law enforcement professionals, your role as negotiators is crucial in maintaining peace and order. Your ability to de-escalate tensions, resolve crises, and protect lives is invaluable. Continue to hone your skills, learn from every experience, and stay committed to ethical and compassionate negotiation practices.

The impact of effective negotiation extends beyond immediate outcomes; it fosters long-term trust and safety within communities. By mastering negotiation methods and tactics, you contribute to a safer, more just society where conflicts are resolved peacefully, and relationships are built on mutual respect and understanding.

Thank you for your dedication and commitment to this vital aspect of law enforcement. May your journey as negotiators be marked by success, growth, and positive change.

www.ingramcontent.com/pod-product-compliance
Lightning Source LLC
Chambersburg PA
CBHW071840210526
45479CB00001B/224